Mattox Foster O

EXPECTING WITH AN **EMPTY** WOMB: A Story of Redemption and Rebirth

by *Mattox Foster O'Bannon*

Mattox Foster O'Bannon

Edited by Jhordynn (318) 406-2249

Published by MADE 4 THIS ™ (318) 406-2249

Cover designed and formatted by

ISBN (paperback):978-1-7348574-7-4

~To my parents, thank you for living and leaving a legacy of faith in the Most High God.

To my siblings, my love for you is endless. Thanks for your continued love and support.

To every woman who has suffered in silence while feeling less than, feeling broken, damaged, or other than what God created you to be, you are more than a relationship, maternal, or social status. You are God's image personified. Fearfully and wonderfully made! Be courageous. Be bold. And believe in the promises yet fulfilled.~

TABLE OF CONTENTS

TABLE OF CONTENTS

Chapter 1
You Go Girl: Cultural Myths and Motherhood Mandates

I remember the day. Not quite the month, but definitely the year. It was a Saturday morning in 1981. I was eleven years old, and I'd awaken to the start of my womanhood. I screamed and called out for my mom. She wasn't home, but my sister-in-law entered the bedroom asking what was wrong.

I said, "I'm bleeding! I'm bleeding! I'm going to die!"

She laughed at me, saying, "Girl, you are not dying; it's just your period."

The dreaded "Aunt Sally", as referred to by me and my five close middle school girl friends, had arrived. I was the third out of our group to start. The three of us all agreed that neither of us liked the cramps, inconvenience, nor the yuckiness of the maturing of our bodies.

Show and Tell

I recall when I saw the episode of The Cosby Show when Rudy started her period and how she felt about it; I can also recall the conversations between myself and my middle school friend girls. Once one started to get our periods, you can imagine the conversations during lunch and at recess. I remember my close friend girls and I talking about the “change” and what happens when you start your period. In our small group of five, the starting of our periods staggered, but it was like show and tell each time one of us started.

“How did you sleep?” “In what position?” “Where were you when you started?” “What does yours look like?” “What kind of pad to use?” “How often do you change?” were all questions the four of us bombarded her with.

Oh, and the myths we shared, thinking them to be true: “Don't sit in water.” “You “have to take showers during your period, not baths.” “Be careful not to cut yourself; you can bleed to death.” “Don't go swimming in the ocean; sharks smell blood and will attack.” “Always wear dark clothing during your period (this proved beneficial).” “Wearing tampons means you are having sex, so you should only carry pads.”

Of course, cramps and what to do about them were always a point of discussion. Imagine these conversations from the minds of pre-teen girls.

I remember entering high school and being told by my mother that if I became pregnant all of my privileges and freedoms would be taken from me. She said at that point I would be considered an adult, and as such, my participation in extracurricular activities would be gone. My extracurricular activities that she was referring to included: playing basketball and softball for my high school team, holding class offices as Vice President and President of my class, going to the Homecoming dance or Prom, and hanging with my friends at the skating rink.

There was an enormity associated with having my cycle and its foray into womanhood. There was heavy teaching that Christian girls keep themselves for their husbands. I was told that men don't want what everybody else has had and that "good girls" keep their legs closed because the good men don't marry loose women.

The older I became, the heavier my cycle became. It would be so heavy and painful. I recall lying in the fetal position underneath that same sister-n-law's (who informed me that I wasn't dying) desk during school hours trying to ease the pain. Doctors advised birth control as an option to alleviate the painful cramps and heaviness; however, the use of birth control was viewed as permission to engage in premarital sex and was frowned upon by Mother.

My parents— though one held a GED and the other a high school diploma— placed an emphasis on and valued education and expected their children to pursue higher education. Consequently, when a couple of my friends became pregnant in high school, I was once again lectured on the expectations that I would complete high school on time, go to college and graduate, then on to law school. I was told to remain focused. "Don't embarrass your family by getting pregnant, especially out of wedlock."

There was unconditional support because I evaded the cardinal sin of Black girlhood: pregnancy. Early pregnancy seemed to be a dream-stealer. The praise I received for not becoming pregnant was always accompanied by a cautionary tale about a bright future which would be later abandoned because of the immediate demands of motherhood. I became so terrified of pregnancy that I developed anxiety at the very anticipation of getting pregnant accidentally.

I became sexually active during college in my mid-twenties, but I was very aware that I didn't want to be an unwed mother. When I graduated college and did not immediately marry, Mom said, "You can go to law school." I never did, but that was the expectation.

Then the conversations after college became, "When are you going to find a nice, saved young man and settle down?" The complete opposite of the prior decades where I was conditioned to keep my legs closed and scolded about what good girls don't do.

There was never a conversation of the amount of time I had to conceive a baby, unless it was, **"Wait!"** Then it became, "What are you waiting on?" "You know your clock is ticking."

I escaped the social stigma surrounding urban teen pregnancy only to bump up against another prevalent issue regarding Black females: uterine fibroids....

Chapter 2
TEASED: BRIDESMAID, NEVER THE BRIDE. "I guess I won't see any grandchildren from you…"

My cycles continued to be heavy in my twenties. At one point I was suspected of having endometriosis, but an exam showed that to not be true. I just wanted answers and a solution to ease my cycles and bring as much comfort as possible.

My OB/GYNs were aware that, though I didn't know when that would be, I was waiting until marriage to have children. However, never once did any of my doctors encourage me to get pregnant because of the "ticking clock" or to consider freezing my eggs since I wasn't married. Most doctors dismissed my reproductive health concerns, having the mindset that I was only in my twenties and had time.

By age thirty, I remained unmarried, not in a long term relationship, and suffering from fibroids. The first time I'd even heard of them was when I was being diagnosed. Not even then was I advised that my time to be able to conceive was "winding up" or that fibroids would impact my ability to have children. I had my first surgery to remove five fibroids at the age of thirty-five.

It was also around that time that I had given up on

being married before having a child. After months of trying to get pregnant with a boyfriend and being unsuccessful, I'd become concerned. I saw a doctor about it, and she suggested a procedure called embolization to shrink my fibroids by blocking off their blood supply; I obliged. I still didn't get pregnant after that. I took pills to increase my fertility; I still didn't get pregnant. Next was to surgically remove the fibroids through a myomectomy. I underwent the surgery, and the fibroids came back. Nothing lasted. After each procedure and surgery, they returned.

Waiting. Seems like all I'd done for months. Waiting for test results, waiting on my body to respond to the various procedures I'd undergone to improve fertility and cycles, waiting for prayers to be answered. Waiting on God.

I'd become a familiar face to the medical staff, some offering a compassionate smile, others an empathetic touch. All sharing the unspoken truth that as much as they'd like to predict or determine treatment results, the only thing any had influence over were the scheduling of appointments and their cheery dispositions.

This one particular day, after checking in at the front desk, I found a seat in the far corner of the room. The waiting room was crowded with couples, expecting women, and me. To pass the time, I began flipping through the latest edition of *Parents* magazine. Articles from experts and parents all weighing in on the correct, convenient, economical, or trendy way of raising children only heightened my anxiety level.

With each passing minute, my heartbeat accelerated and turned the silent ticking of the clock into what felt like an eternity. Hands sweaty and mouth dry, I began to silently recite the Model Prayer. "Our Father, which art in heaven, hallowed be thy name, thy kingdom come thy will be done on earth as it is in heaven. Give us this day...."

The nurse called my name. It was now time to see the doctor for the results. Gathering my things, I took a quick look around while making sure not to leave anything behind. Never realizing my world was about to be turned upside down, and I'd never view the waiting room the same, I finished saying my prayer as I followed the nurse out of the waiting area.

As she led me down the long hallway, the casual conversation of "how are you today" and the obligatory discussion of the weather commenced and ended with, "The doctor will be in to see you shortly." Glancing around her office, I noticed the walls held a varied mixture of nicely framed family portraits, degrees and accreditations, drawings artfully created by little hands with crayons, and several laminated pictures of the reproductive system. Just as I began to daydream of having my own wall filled with collages of family portraits and drawings of stick people, my doctor entered the room.

“Hi. How are you today?” she began, and before I had a chance to answer, she proceeded to compliment the red and black flowered spaghetti strapped blouse I’d worn

As she sat behind her desk, I attempted to read her expression and body language for clues.

“I’m sorry I don’t have good news for you,” is the only thing I remember hearing as she handed me a box of tissues that seemingly appeared out of nowhere.

Her mouth was moving as my heart was breaking. Floodgates of hopelessness, despair, and anguish worked in concert with the tears that cascaded down the face of my bowed head. I couldn’t believe it! Surgery, procedures, treatments, meds, pain, sleepless nights, prayers, tears, pleading with God— nothing worked. Three words turned my world upside down: “**You are infertile**.” My dreams of an idyllic, preplanned life of motherhood and marriage were instantly placed in peril and uncertainty.

The combination of low egg production, fibroids, and age had killed my dreams of pregnancy. Killed my hopes. Killed my dreams. Killed my beliefs. Killed my happiness. Killed my joy.

My body had failed me.

I never thought that I would be unable to conceive. I knew of no one who was infertile. I never heard of a

Black infertile woman or couple. Mother had me at the age of forty-one, one week prior to turning forty-two.

I'd spent a lifetime battling stereotypes only to be hit with one I couldn't defeat: infertility. Studies show that Black women are affected more by infertility than White women—11.5% to their 7% to be exact (according to Dr. Desiree McCarthy-Keith, a Reproductive Endocrinologist at Georgia Reproductive Specialists). I'm a triple minority: Black, woman, and infertile.

The walk from the doctor's office to my car was the longest ever. My steps saddled with the weight of three words playing over and over in my ears was intensified by pamphlets of information on alternatives such as fostering, adoption, and support groups. Although shared with kindness and aims of encouragement, to my arms, it felt like I was carrying fifty pound weights.

I couldn't bear the thought of never bearing children, never experiencing what was supposed to be the natural occurrence that comes with being a woman. Not to mention the feelings of embarrassment and shame! The angst and anxiety of informing my family and my friends literally reminded me of the book written by Nathaniel Hawthorne The Scarlett Letter. Only my letter was "B" for barren, which wore on me like a badge of shame.

I saw infertility as a death sentence; my diagnosis became my garment of death. I wore it like a shroud of black, an attire of mourning always as a reminder of what didn't and wouldn't come naturally for me. A serenade of depressive thoughts synchronized with emotions of unworthiness, undeserving, damaged, unfit to live enveloped my mind and body.

I literally grieved for the loss my fertility; I cried out to God for answers. I felt unloved, unworthy of God's trust with being a mom. I kept asking myself, *How could this be? What did I do*? I said over and over again, *This can't be right,* while confessing every sin and asking for forgiveness in hopes of a mistake, in hopes of a miracle! With the loss of my fertility went my contentment, my joy, my excitement for life. All the dreams and idealistic ambitions tied to a happily ever after life now felt so out of reach and unattainable.

I'd followed the rules the majority of my life. I'd waited and practiced abstinence in obedience to God. I felt duped by all the Christian expressions and phrases "Wait on the Lord" and "God's timing" and "Obedience pays off" that I was taught and digested all of my life.

I felt that I held up my end of the bargain. I was a good girl who wasn't promiscuous, went to church, read and studied my Bible, tried my best to keep the commandments and follow the direction and instructions of a faithful Christian girl like I was taught. I did everything that I was supposed to do all out of obedience and in an effort to maintain the theological standard set for me as a child of being "found".

Check Mark.

Infertile women and couples go through the normal stages of grief: shock/denial, pain and guilt, anger and bargaining, depression, and acceptance. Experts state that the stages are universal and all can spend a different amount of time and/or intensity moving through these stages. However, the five stages may not occur in any specific order.

I know I have experienced the varying stages at different times and honestly feel there are or have been certain triggers that cause me to experience a particular stage or level of grief. For instance, questions or statements like: "What are you waiting on to have a baby?" "When are you going to get pregnant?" "You don't have any kids, yet?" "Maybe it is not God's plan for you to have children for some reason." "You don't want kids?" "Why did you wait so long to try?" "You're lucky. I'd love to have some alone time without my kids!" "You can borrow mine anytime." "Honey, my husband/boyfriend can just look at me and I get pregnant!" "I can't miss a day taking my birth control; even one day can cause me to get pregnant."

Albeit said in jest or concern, each remark makes me feel less and less of a woman and more like damaged goods, prompting the same old questions of *Why me?* At times triggering a level of anxiety that has in the past led to a period of recurring depression, anger, and/or guilt.

People can be sympathetic and openly discuss most illnesses, diseases, or medical conditions and without question offer support, encouragement, etcetera. But to the couple or woman struggling with infertility, there can be a wall of silence and shame. In my experience, it is an awkward conversation. Friends, family, and acquaintances either don't know what to say, don't know how to respond, or the immediate come back is, "Just adopt" or "You can keep my child(ren) any time you want" followed by an innocent chuckle. So, I choose to suffer in silence and just keep it to myself, avoiding all conversations remotely dealing with pregnancy and childbearing. Not many in my family are aware of my struggles, and I've shared this with only one or two of my friends.

Check Mark.

For so long I was angry with God— angry with what appeared to be His unwillingness to grant my desire to bear children. Angry because I felt I'd wasted my years of fertility while waiting on God to answer my prayers for a husband. I felt I sacrificed my fertility, my years of viability, my child bearing years waiting on God, waiting for Him to send my husband to live the covenant life/promise of the Bible. And this time I wanted to rewind the hands of time. I wanted a do over.

What if I could just have a do over in an attempt to restore those things lost in time or opportunity? Oh, to be planning a wedding and then awaiting the arrival of my first child. I wanted my dreams back, my hopes back. I did not want to believe that this normal order of life would not exist for me, especially when the Word of God says children are a blessing. Where is my blessing? Psalm 127:3 states, *"Behold, children are a gift of the LORD, The fruit of the womb is a reward."* Yet, I was faced with these very real possibilities that my lifelong dreams weren't to be.

Like most women, I'd dreamed about my wedding day since I was a little girl playing with dolls and stuffed animals. My variety of Disney Princess dolls dressed in their classic gown regalia played my role as the bride; my collection of teddy bears served as my groom. Baby Alive, My Little Pony, Strawberry Shortcake, and a number of Weebles were the wedding guests.

Even as an adolescent, I was ever mindful of my expected role as a wife and mother. I'd played "house" with my dolls and stuffed animals, using my Easy Bake Oven and toy stove to prepare meals and mud pies for my husband and children.

I vividly remember pleading with my mother to allow me to stay up late to watch the royal wedding of Princess Diana and Prince Charles in 1981. I watched as a wide eyed eleven year old girl fascinated by the pageantry of it all! The following school week was filled with conversations among my pre-teen girl friends about her dress, the train, the veil, her tiara. Wow, that tiara! Who didn't want to become a princess? To marry a prince in a cathedral with thousands of people watching and to afterwards be whisked away in a horse drawn carriage?

My imagining went to debating with my teenage friends about which heart throb crush would be better suited for our plans of marriage and the importance of picking the right color and styles for bride's maid dresses. By that point in my life, I'd attended or served in enough weddings as hostess or junior bridesmaid to know that taffeta and green were out for my choices!

My plans only intensified with age. Paid subscriptions to *Brides* and *Martha Stewart Weddings* magazines provided plenty of inspiration and expertise to fill a binder of plans outlining invitations, escort cards, seating arrangements, meal choices, buffet, seated or passed hors d'oeuvres, wedding times—mid day or evening, destination wedding, event spaces, flowers—real or fake, wedding dresses off the shoulder, scalloped neck, long, short, veil or no veil, reception decor, band or DJ, gift registry, etcetera, all based on my vivid dreams and the latest popular trends.

The older I became, the more I yearned and desired to have a husband and family. It was never a thought that I would not be married and not have children at this point in my life. The longer the wait, and with each failed relationship, my faith became like waves of an ocean coming in at high tide, strong and forceful, ready and willing to take on anything in its way. And other times as feeble and weak after being beaten and battered by the seemingly constant up and down, in and out emotional roller coaster attached to an insatiable— at times overbearing— longing for marriage and motherhood.

One day while reflecting on my high school memory book— you know the ones that ask you to list where you will be in ten years— I recall writing my life plans boldly in ink. I wrote I'd return to my high school reunion living the life of a corporate attorney, married with 2.5 children, driving a BMW, and living the up and coming suburbia lifestyle of someone whose life goals and dreams had become reality.

Instead, by my ten year class reunion, none of anything I'd written or projected was my reality. I wasn't an attorney, never even went to law school, hadn't married, no children to speak of, was driving a Toyota, and living nowhere close to the suburbs. Needless to say, I didn't attend my ten year high school reunion, nor any of the subsequent decades following.

Chapter 3
Church Baby

I grew up in the church. I was what you could call a "church baby". My parents were active in ministry and church activities and expected me to be as well. There was Sunday School, regular Sunday morning service, Bible Training Union (BTU), evening services, Wednesday night Bible Study, and other church activities that I was involved with all of my childhood and most of my adult life.

The church is a place in our culture where marriage and kids are promoted and expected; as such, church is a good place to find marital support, but it isn't always a source of refuge for the childless. Singles are often met with questions about when they will get married and unnecessarily pitied or prayed for when a potential spouse isn't in the picture. Whereas young couples are bombarded with, "Isn't it time the two of you start having kids?" as if it is like scheduling a tune-up for your car, and their marriage doesn't really matter until a child validates it.

As a single woman, I held true to what the Apostle Paul said in 1 Corinthians chapter 7 that singles should give their life to the church as that is their primary concern. So, I kept busy with ministry work, commitments, and leadership roles. Making myself available and open to the numerous activities and programs, telling myself this is my focus and season of single commitment. All while believing and trusting the scriptures that state, "He who finds a wife finds a good thing" and "Children are a blessing from God".

Yet, as time went on, that didn't become my existence. I was neither married nor a mother. Where was my promised life? The life I dreamt of since a little girl, the role I had rehearsed over and over in my young imagination and prepared and prayed for in my adulthood. Never expected or planned for anything less. But as life would have it, I became the very thing I fought against most of my life: becoming a number, a statistic, a check mark inside a box.

I am fairly familiar with many of the Biblical characters and stories of the Bible. Like most, I heard the accounts of their lives preached and taught throughout my lifetime and had developed a particular appreciation for the women of the Bible. And of course, as a woman, I found many of their life events relatable, but none more than Sarai, the wife of Abraham; Hannah, the wife of Elkanah; the widow of Zarephath; and the mother and daughter-in-law duo Naomi and Ruth. Accounts of their lives and faith struggles resonated with me in various stages of my life, but even more personally after my diagnosis and my desire for motherhood.

First, let's discuss the Old Testament. There is a story of Elijah and the widow of Zarephath. There was a famine in the land (more details on that later), and the widow and her son were on the verge of starvation when God told Elijah to go to the city of Zidon in the ancient Middle East where he had prepared a widow to take care of him. Upon his arrival, he met the widow who was gathering sticks to build a fire and asked her to prepare him something to eat. She explained they had nothing left to eat but "a handful of meal in a barrel and a little oil in cruse", and she was preparing that as their last meal.

"13 And Elijah said unto her, Fear not; go and do as thou hast said: but make me thereof a little cake first, and bring it unto me, and after make for thee and for thy son. 14 For thus saith the LORD God of Israel, The barrel of meal shall not waste, neither shall the cruse of oil fail, until the day that the LORD sendeth rain upon the earth. 15 And she went and did according to the saying of Elijah: and she, and he, and her house, did eat many days. 16 And the barrel of meal wasted not, neither did the cruse of oil fail, according to the word of the LORD, which he spake by Elijah" (1 Kings 17:13-16) (KJV).

The widow of Zarephath trusted the man of God and his word that she would be blessed through her obedience and faith, in such she was rewarded! Elijah remained with the widow and her son, and the Lord sustained them through the famine for three years. We can surmise the widow was possibly dealing with a variety of emotions, fears, and feelings; yet, her desperation still yielded hope, and she gave willingly of her last at great risk. She believed what Elijah said that if she made him a piece of cake first that her oil and flour would not run out until the famine was ended. Her faith was compensated, and instead of one last meal for her and her son, there were many more meals.

Just as we've noticed with the widow, the battle between fear and faith is one every woman of God experiences in her lifetime. Whether we're dealing with an illness of a love one, loss of employment, experiencing problems in our marriage, the behavior of a wayward child, financial problems, etcetera, we have to remind ourselves that these occurrences have not taken God by surprise. He is aware of it, and He can do something about it. But if His ultimate will is not to change your situation but to grow your faith through it, trusting in His sovereignty and growing in His likeness is God's purpose for your life.

Chapter 4
Bitterness of Soul

The Bible is replete with accounts of women who in one season or another of their lives waited on God for long periods of time for answered prayers and for a child. Sarai beyond the age of childbearing laughed and doubted; Rebecca questioned the reason for her struggle in relation to the promise of God. Rachel said to Jacob, "Give me children or else I die." Hannah pleaded with God. Sampson's mom was barren and childless. Elizabeth was also beyond the age for natural childbearing when she became pregnant with John the Baptist.

Barrenness for women in Biblical times was much like it is for many women today. It can be a very painful, isolating experience. Much of a woman's worth, security, and identity in Biblical times and culture was based upon her ability to bear children, specifically male children. Children were viewed as a sign of God's blessings, and consequently being barren was seen as an indication of God's disfavor, which often led to social scorn and ridicule. Male children were viewed and valued as the ones to carry on the family name and to take care of the women in the family; they were particularly expected to take care of their widowed mother. Again, much like today, the real state of mind of the couple or woman experiencing infertility is influenced by their environment. Just as in those days, the very problem facing women can be attributed to the culture and beliefs of their society.

In ancient times, a man who had no son could adopt a servant as his heir or take a second wife or concubine to produce an heir. A wife was obligated to have children. If she could not, she was required to be open to the very real possibility of her husband taking another wife or servant to secure an heir.

As such was the example of Abram and Sarai. Responding in fear to the length of time it was taking for the promise from God that she would bear a son to manifest, she offered her handmaid Hagar to her husband Abram. She probably felt that giving him an heir through another woman (which, again, was the custom of the time) was more bearable than waiting on God's timing. At this point, it had been ten years since God made the promise to Abram that he would become a father of nations. "And Sarai said unto Abram, *'Behold now, the Lord hath restrained me from bearing: I pray thee, go in unto my maid; it may be that I may obtain children by her.'* And Abram listened to the voice of Sarai" (Genesis 16:2).

The Bible states Sarai waited for twenty-five years before she could bring forth a seed in accordance to God's plan. Why will people who have devoted their life, men and women who love and honor Him, and whose strength and faith lies in God and God alone face such a test of faith from God who they believe and trust? Remember, the Bible says, "THE LORD HATH RESTRAINED ME FROM BEARING" (Genesis 16:2).

Personal experience will fail me if I attempt to explain explicitly what Sarai and Abram endured and the depth of their distress while waiting for God's promise for thirty years. Yet, they were crowned hero and heroine of faith because of their complete reliance upon the promises of God irrespective of how long it took. The barrenness of Sarai never led Abram to question the authority of God nor doubt his faith in God. And as such, Abram staggered not, and what God said was fulfilled. There may have been times when he had to remind himself of what God spoke to him all those years ago. Yet, he faltered not, but believed steadfast in these words.

Hebrew 6:13-15: *"* ***13*** *For when God made promise to Abraham, because he could swear by no greater, he sware by himself,* ***14*** *Saying, Surely blessing I will bless thee, and multiplying I will multiply thee.* ***15*** *And so, after he had patiently endured, he obtained the promise" (NLT).* Even though the name Abraham is used, the Bible is referring to Abram. God changed Abram's name to Abraham to confirm His promise to Abram. God changed Sarai's name to Sarah to confirm His promise to her as well.

Sarai held on to these words: "Be fruitful and multiply". Imagine how many times she repeated this to herself or reminded God of His own words, while believing that they are life giving and have the power to refute the report of her own body. However, like many of us along this faith journey, maybe Sarai needed reassurance from her husband that *he* still believed in the promise of God (remember she laughed when God told Abram she would bear him an heir. So, there may have been a slight matter of unbelief on Sarai's part).

Thirteen years later, God reminded Abram of his promise to make him a father of generations (with this reminder, God changed their names from Abram to Abraham and Sarai to Sarah). Sarai was ninety, and Abram was one hundred when their son Isaac was born. God's promises are faithful even when we are not; He exhibited this three times with Abraham and Sarah, even when they chose to help God out or responded in fear instead of faith. God initially told Abram when Sarai was sixty-five that she would bear him a son. Ten years later when she was seventy-five, He reminded Abram of this promise. Thirteen years when she was eighty-nine, God told them again, and Sarah gave birth to Isaac at the age of ninety.

Rebecca and Isaac waited twenty years. Rachel experienced a long period of barrenness. We aren't told exactly how long Hannah waited, but we know she was desperately seeking God during the time of their annual pilgrimage to sacrifice at the temple in Shiloh, and she was in such despair that she sought to separate herself from her husband and to seek the Lord for a child.

How do you blend your grief, pain, and anguish with your belief in God and His promises? Even when you know without a doubt that He loves you and that all things work together for the good of them who love the Lord and are called according to his purpose? Why do you hold on when thousand-year-old promises on thin parchment paper are the only balm to soothe your aching heart? One syllable four letter word is all I have to offer: HOPE.

It takes hope, prayer, perseverance, and an understanding of what's on the other side of waiting, hence when you realize what's on the other side of endurance, the waiting doesn't become something you dread, resent, or rush through. You begin to see it as a part of the process of the promise, and your willingness to surrender your will to God's WILL positions you to receive your reward for faithfulness.

Listen, I had to learn this the hard way, through years of fighting, running, and allowing my pain and trauma to turn me away from God. Allowing the perception of who I wasn't influence who I am and who I was designed to be, I only saw myself through the lens of loss until I learned my why.

You can discover yours also by meditating on the scriptures and allowing them to be a constant reminder of why you haven't given up, why you have hope against all odds despite life's trials. Let the Word of God be a constant reminder that you are not alone. That what seems or even feels like rejection now is preparing you for your destiny.

EMPTY WOMB D
DISCUSSION

EXPECTING WITH AN EMPTY WOMB

STRONG GRACE
NOT FORSAKEN HOPE
LOVED CHOSEN
BEAUTIFUL DELIGHTED
NOT ASHAMED

Mattox Foster O'Bannon

How do you cope with being a servant of God, when He doesn't give you a YES to the one thing you were created to do? In Expecting With An Empty Womb, we are taken on Ms. Foster's journey and struggles with infertility, Christianity, faith, and hope. We will discover and discuss how God gave her the necessary "Yes" to complete His purpose and plans for her life.

27

EBR Parish Jones
Branch Libra
Conference
6222 Jones Cr
225-756-1

*This event is not sponsored
EBR Parish Library

'EXPECTING WITH AN

' BOOK

AUTHOR
MEET & GREET
SAT AUGUST
@ 3:30

Deuteronomy 31:8 (KJV), *"And the LORD, he it is that doth go before thee; he will be with thee, he will not fail thee, neither forsake thee: fear not, neither be dismayed."*

Psalms 147:3 (KJV), *" He healeth the broken in heart, and bindeth up their wounds."*

Psalm 34:18 (NLT), *"The LORD is close to the brokenhearted; he rescues those whose spirits are crushed."*

Chapter 5
Blessed are Those That Mourn

Scripture says, "Blessed are they that mourn for they shall be comforted." While reading this scripture, I was thinking, *How is mourning a blessing*? Mourning is typically associated with grief, loss, death, and sadness. How can any of those descriptions connote blessings which I equate with happiness, life, etcetera? How does God expect me to feel blessed in my mourning? What is it He's trying to teach me, to accomplish in me during this time?

I'm reminded of the Old Testament figure Naomi who returned to Judah with her two daughters in law after the death of her husband Elimelech and two sons Mahlon and Chilion. The narrative opens with the family moving to Moab due to a famine in their homeland of Judah. They resided there over a course of ten years. During which time Naomi's husband dies, and she is left with her two sons. They marry Moabite women Orpah and Ruth; however, both of her sons die without children. Naomi goes from wife and mother to widow and childless. Two of the most significant identifiers in the culture of her time, wife and mother, have been stripped from her identity.

Upon hearing that the Lord had restored food and the famine had ended, Naomi decides it is time to return home. She and her daughters in law begin their journey back to Judah filled with grief and uncertainty. Naomi was so downhearted that she encouraged her daughters in law Orpah and Ruth three times to return to their families and offered the blessing of the Lord upon them for their kindness to her. However, her daughters in law cry and insist upon continuing, pleading with her not to make them leave. Naomi seeks to discourage them, expressing she had nothing remaining to offer them: no husband to impregnate her and especially no additional sons for them to marry. Describing her situation, Naomi determines that the "hand of the Lord is gone out against me". Being convinced of what Naomi was saying, Orpah returned to her family and home. As such, Ruth was the only one to continue on to Judah with Naomi.

Upon arriving in Judah, and as she was greeted by the women of the town, Naomi explained how she felt. She expressed how the Lord had dealt bitterly with her due to the loss of her husband and sons. Naomi informed them that she no longer wanted to be called Naomi (which means my pleasant one) but Mara (which means bitter).

Much like Naomi felt, we assume or feel that God has dealt bitterly with us during the death of spouse, parent, or child; divorce, dislocation, loss of a job, illness, disease. All of these can trigger us to question whether God is punishing us or has forgotten about His child. Pain and trials can cause one to become blind to the presence of God and shifts our focus. The enemy will try to make you feel abandoned, discarded, and alone.

In instances like these, we have to hold on to the very promises of God. II Corinthians 4:8-9 states, *"[8] We are hard-pressed on every side, yet not crushed; we are perplexed, but not in despair; [9] persecuted, but not forsaken; struck down, but not destroyed."* Even Isaiah 41:10 reminds us of God's presence: *"Don't be afraid, for I am with you. Don't be discouraged, for I am your God. I will strengthen you and help you. I will hold you with my victorious right hand."* We are never alone; cast all of your cares on Him— I Peter 5:7.

We have in our heavenly Father someone who can relate to your every need. He has suffered, He has mourned, and He has been rejected. Because of His experiences, you are not alone. You are not alone in your feelings, and you are not alone in your grief. Jesus sees, He knows, and He cares about you.

Because Naomi and Ruth had no husbands or sons to take care of them, and thus no source of income, they were reliant upon the laws of Deuteronomy pertaining to gleaning and harvesting. They were also reliant upon the laws pertaining to that of the kinsman redeemer. According to the dictionary, a redeemer is someone who buys back, recovers, pays off, or exchanges something for goods.

Deuteronomy declares once an owner of the field gathered what was harvested the first time, he should leave some for the poor and strangers to glean. In other words, don't take all the olives off the branches, don't take all the wheat from the fields, and leave some remaining for those in need. This was again God's way of taking care and providing for widows, and those who were destitute or poor.

Ruth was a Moabite from Moab— a Paganist society— and was also a widow with no children, but she truly loved her mother in law Naomi. So much so that she converted and consecrated her life to God and Naomi. Ruth wanted not only to be with Naomi; she wanted her relationship with Jehovah. She knew Naomi was not a Pagan. The Bible doesn't provide background on their life in Moab, but it can be deduced that Naomi and her husband Elimelech continued to serve and worship God while in a strange land. Hence Ruth noticed and wanted this enough to leave her family, culture, and religious practices. She told Naomi, *"16 ... 'Don't ask me to leave you and turn back. Wherever you go, I will go; wherever you live, I will live. Your people will be my people, and your God will be my God. 17 Wherever you die, I will die, and there I will be buried. May the Lord punish me severely if I allow anything but death to separate us'" (Ruth 1:16-17)!*

Ruth's commitment to the ways, beliefs, and her love for Naomi became a testament to those in Judah. Everyone became aware of her willingness to care for her including a near kinsman relative named Boaz who rewarded Ruth by allowing protection and provision while she gathered from his fields. Boaz instructed his servants to not only allow Ruth to gather grain among the piles that were already harvested, but to not reproach her and to leave extra on the stalks. In a single day, Ruth had enough to eat and more to take to share with Naomi. What a blessing! This was the laws of Deuteronomy in action.

Again, recall how Naomi felt. She was consumed by what she had lost more than what she had remaining. She, like many of us, permit our accomplishments, status, material acquirements to define and dictate our value and identity. In focusing solely on her despair and what she no longer had, Naomi became distracted. Distracted from the realization that her faith, her relationship, and a belief that Jehovah would provide was the greatest thing she had to offer. Yet in her hurt, she encouraged Ruth and Orpah to return to their families in Moab because she believed she had nothing else to offer them. She could not give them more husbands, and she felt she was too old to remarry (Ruth 1:11-13). Again, while only considering what she had lost and what she no longer was, she discounted the wisdom, good judgment and teachings that still remained. It wasn't until later that she understood the intangibles, (the attributes and aspects of Christ) such as love, compassion, faith, and hope are priceless, and these are the greatest things any of us have to offer our children, family, and friends.

But thankfully, though Naomi didn't recognize these characteristics as valuable at the time, Ruth did, and her refusal to leave Naomi is evident that she wanted what Naomi couldn't see through the darkness of her circumstances.

As we continue, let's bear in mind Naomi's return to Judah was due to her hearing of the Lord restoring food to the inhabitants of his chosen city Judah. Yet the same rationale she had given Orpah and Ruth to go back to their families were the same type circumstances she was under in returning to Judah.

I find that rather ironic. So, my question is who was she relying on to take care of her upon her arrival in Judah? Remember she felt so forgotten and forsaken by God that she changed her name from Naomi to Mara. She only saw one way to resolve their problems; she could not see any other way out. But that is the beauty of the God we serve. His ways are not our ways; His thoughts are not our thoughts (Isaiah 55:9). God already had a plan; He was already preparing the way. He just needed a willing participant with an open heart to seek and serve Him, and He found it in Ruth.

Through the marriage of Boaz and Ruth came the lineage of Jesus Christ, our kinsman redeemer. Through God's grace and restoration and Naomi's testimony, Ruth came to know God. God restored Ruth and Naomi and gave them a son and a grandson. Ruth was rewarded for her faith and support, and Naomi was considered blessed among her people "more than anyone with seven sons".

But let us consider if Naomi had missed the chance to witness and share the provision of God with Ruth because she was attempting to push her away through her pain and grief? What if she had stayed in the state of mind that gripped her with fear, grief, and bitterness when she returned to Judah? As opposed to realizing God's provision in the Kinsman Redeemer Boaz and in teaching Ruth what to do and essentially how to trust God and His will? Imagine the possibility of Naomi returning to Judah alone if Ruth had not persisted and ignored her initial suggestion that she return to her own people?

Just as our trials and life's affairs can place us in a position of questioning whether God has forgotten about us and our hearts' desires, we must hold on to the strength of God's love as a comfort to us when we call out to him. We stretch our hands out to Him as His children, and He is faithful to not only hear our prayers but to answer them.

As the book of James states: *"2 Count it all joy my brothers, whenever you experience various trials, 3 knowing that the testing of your faith produces endurance. 4 But endurance must do its complete work, so that you may be mature and complete, lacking nothing...12 A man who endures trials is blessed, because when he passes the test he will receive the crown of life that God has promised to those who love him." (*James 1:2-4, 12 HSCB Version). God always has a plan and purpose for our pain.

Deuteronomy 31:8, "And the Lord, He is the One who goes before you. He will be with you, He will not leave you nor forsake you; do not fear nor be dismayed."

Chapter 6
Identity Crisis

For a period of time, Naomi was going through an identity crisis. Her pain and grief caused her to forget who and whose she was. I know that I have definitely gone through periods of time where I forgot who and whose I was; there have been times when I didn't even know or like who was in the mirror staring back at me.

When the voice of doubt is loud like a train whistling down the tracks warning oncoming cars that danger lurks at the next railroad crossing, resonating louder than that of the still small voice of God... especially when the world/society reminds us constantly about our ticking biological clock— we're bombarded with commercials for ovulation tests and pregnancy tests... questions from well-intended friends and family about when will we have children or why don't we want children… invitations to baby showers, weddings, birth announcements, etcetera…

When worldly definitions of worth and value differ from what the Word of God says… when your maternal or marriage status, profession, education, race, economic standing is warring with Psalms 45:1, with the sacrifice of the Cross, with the love of God…

When shame slips in with the silent words unspoken as another month begins and ends, pregnant only with hope… when silence gives shame all the voice it needs to whisper silently, "Something is wrong with you" and "God is displeased with you"… **what do you do?**

It is amazing the amount of silence surrounding the struggles of infertility. The silence of avoidance of any and everything dealing with pregnancy. The silence of wanting to talk, but being scared of what others will say and think. The silence of trying to avoid the one thing you are consumed with wondering and worried about. The silence of your own thoughts dominated by questions of why and what ifs.

Infertility made me feel broken, isolated, ostracized, embarrassed, less than… All these feelings of emptiness are fueled by society, family expectations, and my thoughts of regret. Constantly bombarded and reminded about what I did not have, , seeing pregnant women everywhere I looked, comparing myself to them, my accomplishments— which in my mind was nothing compared to my inability to conceive. Nothing else mattered.

It was of no consequence that I was educated, well liked, owned my home, traveled some, and viewed by friends as having it all together. It was never enough. My measuring stick was always associated with a procedure or the blue indicator line on a home pregnancy test. Those became my standards of worth, success, happiness, and validation. And with each failed attempt, I was reminded of my lack, of what I did not have, of my maternal status, and thus of what I was.

Barren.

But one encounter with the Master of the universe, with the Lord Almighty, we can become whole, filled, joyful, and restored. Hannah was a woman grieved by her barrenness, provoked and taunted by Peninah, her husband's other wife, because of such. Remember in ancient Israel, children were an indication of blessings and obedience to the Lord.
"6 *And her adversary also provoked her sore, for to make her fret, because the Lord had shut up her womb.*
7 And as he did so year by year, when she went up to the house of the Lord, so she provoked her; therefore she wept, and did not eat." (1 Samuel 1:6-7)

Yearly, she and her husband and family would journey to the temple in Shiloh to offer a sacrifice to the Lord. Her husband, albeit very supportive in offering her a double portion to sacrifice, didn't understand her strong desire for a son. "Am I not better than seven sons?" he asked. It's not that Hannah didn't love her husband and was not satisfied with his efforts to show how he valued her as his wife, but she desired more. She was grateful, yet unfulfilled, and her only recourse was to take her deferred dreams and place them at the foot of the Master.

After offering her sacrifice to the Lord, Hannah kneeled in prayer. A prayer so heartfelt, distressful, and emotional that her lips moved, but no voice was heard. Her prayer, albeit silent, spoke of a vow to God that if He blessed her with a male child, she would give him to the Lord all the days of his life. 1 Samuel 1:11, "*And she vowed a vow, and said, O Lord of hosts, if thou wilt indeed look on the affliction of thine handmaid, and remember me, and not forget thine handmaid, but wilt give unto thine handmaid a man child, then I will give him unto the Lord all the days of his life, and there shall no razor come upon his head.*"

However, the priest Eli thought she was drunk with wine and scolded her. [15] "*And Hannah answered and said, No, my lord, I am a woman of a sorrowful spirit: I have drunk neither wine nor strong drink, but have poured out my soul before the Lord.*"[16]" *Count not thine handmaid for a daughter of Belial: for out of the abundance of my complaint and grief have I spoken hitherto.*" (1 Samuel 1:15-16)

I can recall during another low point of my journey, after receiving some disappointing test results, crying out of my despair and pain to the Lord. I was literally on my knees at the church altar pouring out my anguish, fear, and feelings of rejection to the Lord. A range of emotions from praying and crying and pleadings and wailing were dispersed in between instances where I could only moan. Words left me; I had nothing left to offer but my tears and silent grief.

It is in those moments that I must thank God for knowing my heart, and for His power to decipher my desires and needs.

Isn't it a blessing to have the assurance that God knows what we need in the moment we need it without having to utter a word? That's the trust and peace Hannah received that day in the temple. She was comforted by knowing that God heard her earnest pleas and the knowledge of that changed her entire outlook on her situation.

King David also expressed his feelings of loneliness and doubt of God's presence in the book of Psalms. Psalms 22:1, *"My God, My God, why have You forsaken Me? Why are You so far from helping Me, And from the words of My groaning?"*

Elijah hid in a cave when he was in despair, wanting to die, dealing with fear and what he considered failure. God met him in his deepest, loneliest place. God met him and nourished his physical body and spirit by reminding Elijah that He had not left him, that He was still God and aware of his situation. Not only did God show Elijah that He was aware, but he did something about it. *1 Kings 17:4, God said to Elijah, "You will drink from the brook, and I have directed the ravens to supply you with food there." 1 Kings 17: 6 "The ravens brought [Elijah] bread and meat in the evening..."*

Reflect upon this situation. This is not the first time God has reminded you that you are His, that He is aware of your situation. I realize infertility is a difficult life situation to deal with. I know the feelings of loneliness, distraught, despair, disappointment, questioning, judgement, and condemnation you feel. How the burden of wanting to bear a child can be overwhelming. How everything reminds you of what you don't have. The burning desire to feel the weight of pregnancy, the kick of a child in the womb, to hear the heartbeat of your unborn child, to hold a child of your own in your arms, to share with the world your blessing.

Believe me, I know all too well! I've lived in this cave by the brook that has dried up for years, and I use the word "lived" loosely. I merely existed, only able to take shallow breaths because breathing deeply felt unfair. Laughing, dreaming, hoping, and planning a future all seemed futile because I wasn't fruitful.

How could I be alive? How could I be considered a living, breathing woman but unable to bring life into the world? Much like Elijah, I wanted to die. I felt like I should die. I was tired of fighting, tired of waiting, tired of asking. I questioned my worth, my vitality, my purpose for being, for existing! Why am I here, Lord? Why am I on this earth as a woman if I can't do what you created me to do?

I pleaded, negotiated, bargained for the pain, the laboring, the inconvenience, the discomfort of pregnancy, the sleepless nights, the worry, and the responsibility of parenthood knowing it would all be worth it. I'd trade in sleeping eight hours a night for the 3:00 am feedings. I'll gladly trade my Coach, Dooney & Burke purses for diaper bags. *I'm willing, Lord.*

I had to purge those thoughts and seeds of doubts and focus on the blessings that surrounded me daily, remembering the goodness of God and learn to lean into my faith. Remember you are still a child of God! Nothing or no one can separate you from His love (Romans 8:31-39). The source of your identity is in Christ Jesus, not your role as a mother, business woman, single woman, wife, etcetera, but in Christ. It is our relationship with the Father that defines who and whose we are.

The enemy will attempt to make you feel less than, devalued, damaged, discounted, etcetera. But the love of Christ and His divine purpose for your life is not based upon your ability to birth children, in being a wife, a mogul, successful, wealthy, or your role in life. None of it makes you more or less than. It is this truth, this standard that we should measure and reflect the image of ourselves upon.

I get it. I can relate. Circumstances, trials, and the harsh reality of life all have a tendency to distort what we see and our beliefs. As a result, we fall prey to the lies the enemy has so craftily woven into our thoughts.

Your identity is who God says you are: beautiful, redeemed, reborn, and safe in the hands of God, never to be forsaken or forgotten. Instead of a garment of shame, fear, self-loathing, and lies of the enemy, put on the "garment of salvation" and the cloak of righteousness that are given to us as daughters of the Most High. You are uniquely designed, chosen, and loved by the Creator of the universe who made you in His image. Ask God to help you see yourself through His eyes, through His love and sacrifice. To show you your true identity.

Even now in moments filled with grief and despair and where only my heart speaks for me, I have learned to allow the unfailing love and promise of His presence to speak and comfort me like nothing else can. I say a silent prayer, go to the scriptures, and remind myself that regardless of how I may feel at the time, I am still a daughter of the Most High. I am not forgotten. I am not forsaken.

The Word of God in Philippians 4:6-8 says, "[6] Be
anxious for nothing, but in everything by prayer and
supplication, with thanksgiving, let your requests be
made known to God; [7] *and the peace of God, which*
surpasses all understanding, will guard your hearts
and minds through Christ Jesus. [8] *Finally, brethren,*
whatever things are true, whatever things are noble, whatever things are just, whatever things are pure, whatever things are lovely, whatever things are of good report, if there is any virtue and if there is anything praiseworthy—meditate on these things." (NKJV)

John 14:27: "*Peace I leave with you, My peace I give to you; not as the world gives do I give to you. Let not your heart be troubled, neither let it be afraid.*" (NKJV)

Pastor Rick Warren says, "The deepest level of worship is praising God in spite of pain, thanking God during a trial, trusting Him when tempted, surrendering while suffering, and loving Him when He seems distant." (Purpose Driven Life)

Psalms 43:5: "*Why are you cast down, O my soul? And why are you disquieted within me? Hope in God; For I shall yet praise Him, The help of my countenance and my God.*" (NKJV)

Chapter 7
Beauty for Ashes… Scars from the Journey

I have scars. Scars that remind me of the pain I've endured in an attempt to conceive and birth a child. Physical scars from surgeries and setbacks. Scars long and thick on my lower abdomen from a surgical scapula in my years' long battle with fibroids. Fibroids, much like weeds, keep growing and returning to my uterus. And emotional scars that aren't as visible but are just as prominent. I still cry at times after seeing a commercial or billboard along the city streets advertising motherhood, or while out shopping seeing an expectant woman.

Then there are what I like to call emotional scars: the type tattooed on my heart and mind from embarrassment, discomfort, self-consciousness, inadequacy. Scars like an open womb that don't seem to heal, yet are a reminder of the pain I endure in an attempt to conceive and birth a child.

Over time I've learned to surrender these insecurities to God. So please know I am in no way jealous of women who have been successful at pregnancy, nor do I wish ill will upon them. Though there are times when I wrestle with the desire and yearn to hold a newborn in my arms after hours of laboring to bring the gift of life into the world. My prayer has become, "Father, help me to let go of the disappointment of expectations of myself and that of others that cause me to feel like something is wrong with me. Help me to live in who you created me to be and the purpose and plan you have for my life."

In doing so, I've discovered the tenets of my faith—those intangibles such as love, compassion, faith, and hope have become very important in coping with infertility. They've become my "why". My relationship with the Father and my faith in His love for me have become my source and the "why" I haven't succumbed to the voices and feelings surrounding my diagnosis. His love and guidance are the reasons I am able to share my testimony and journey.

Let's again discuss the widow of Zarephath whom the prophet Elijah stayed with during the three years of the famine. She was a Gentile living in a pagan idol worshipping land; a woman of faith who exchanged her last meal for hope. She had enough faith to believe and trust Elijah that if she used the last bit of flour and oil to prepare his cake first, her flour and oil would not run out during the time of the famine.

Note again she was a Gentile living among the Israelites, and the cause of the famine was due to the Israelite's disobedience in worshipping idol gods which in turn led to their spiritual decay.

Being misled by his wife Jezebel, scripture says Ahab did more to provoke the anger of God than all the kings of Israel before him. 1 Kings 16:30-33 states,
[30]*And Ahab the son of Omri did evil in the sight of the*

Lord above all that were before him. [31]And it came to pass, as if it had been a light thing for him to walk in the sins of Jeroboam the son of Nebat, that he took to wife Jezebel the daughter of Ethbaal king of the Zidonians, and went and served Baal, and worshipped him. [32]And he reared up an altar for Baal in the house of Baal, which he built in Samaria. [33] And Ahab made a grove; and Ahab did more to provoke the Lord God of Israel to anger than all the kings of Israel that were before him.

Though the Bible explicitly speaks against idol worship, King Ahab and Queen Jezebel were the principal figures in leading the children of Israel into worshipping and building altars to Baal. Baal was a Canaanite god and was considered the god of storms and thus of fertility, and the rain she supposedly sent watered the crops and provided a bountiful harvest.

Exodus 20:3-5 states, [3] *"You shall have no other gods before Me. [4] "You shall not make for yourself a carved image—any likeness of anything that is in heaven above, or that is in the earth beneath, or that is in the water under the earth; [5] you shall not bow down to them nor [b]serve them. For I, the LORD your God, am a jealous God, visiting[c] the iniquity of the fathers upon the children to the third and fourth generations of those who hate Me."*

After some time, and while Elijah remained in the widow of Zarephath's home, her son became ill and died. She was upset with Elijah and God asking, "Did you come to remind me of my sin and kill my son?" The death of the son was a tragic and devastating event to the widow. Remember in Biblical times a son was considered very valuable, and a widow's son was her hope for the future. The expectation was that her son would grow and provide for her in her old age.

Now that expectation of her future was shattered. I'm sure she thought, "Why did God preserve my life and the life of my son, only to see him die now, *after* the famine has passed? I was obedient and did as the prophet asked three years ago. This is the thanks I get! Look what YOUR God has brought upon me. Without my son, there will be no one to care for me when I am too old to take care of myself. It's not fair, Prophet! It's not fair, God! Have you come only to tease me and then to bring punishment upon me for some great sin?"

I took this dim view, that my past sins had caused my infertility. That for some reason I was being judged, and my punishment was brought about due to some unconfessed sin. This is a common reaction, but maybe God used this as an opportunity for the Gentile woman to know who He truly is. Maybe He needed to make it personal for her. Sometimes God has to get our attention more than once.

Being a woman marginalized by her widowhood and while living in a pagan society, she could have taken on the view of "when things go well, the gods are with me, and when they don't, the gods are angry with me, and hardship and consequence come as a result of sin". However, the question remains: was her faith really in God? Yes, she had obeyed the prophet of God and had done everything in her power to see to it that God's will was done, but had she truly given her heart over to Him?

Even though she had lived through a three year famine that was the result of idol worship, as a Gentile woman, she and her son were still sustained, and there was no lack in her household. Yet, she still did not know the one true God for herself; she only knew of Him through Elijah. So, her assertion that God was punishing her by the death of her son is wrong thinking but could be attributed to lack of knowledge of God's sovereignty in a society that was worshipping idol gods and killing prophets of the God of Israel.

Point to consider? We are so quick to forget or overlook all the benefits we have received from the Lord when things don't go our way or the way we planned. We often ask, "Why me, Lord? What did I do to deserve this? Where has your blessing gone? Have you forgotten about me? Am I to remain alone forever?"

This is how I felt dealing with infertility. The range of emotions from hope to hopeless from expectation to despair. These are the very same questions I asked God. Albeit a common reaction, God is not a vengeful god. He has no desire to see you suffering. Like any good father, it breaks His heart when His children are hurting, and the misconception that hardship and consequence all come as a result of sin is wrong thinking. Yes, it is true that sin can cause a rift between us and God, but His Word says nothing can separate those of us who have accepted Him as our Lord and Savior. We are sealed and remain in His hand.

Elijah took her son and cried out to the Lord and stretched himself over the boy three times. Elijah prayed with great heart and intimacy with God asking the Lord to restore the child to life. He brought this seemingly inexplicable tragedy to God in prayer. Elijah asked God, "Did you bring me here to bring tragedy upon the widow and her son?" Elijah invited God in and asked Him to intervene. And in His almighty power and through His faithful love, God heard Elijah's prayer and restored the child's life.

The widow's response was, "***Now*** I know you are a man of God." WHY not when the oil and flour did not run out and God fed them for three years? It's human nature to believe upon seeing, to have some tangible evidence, to expect a guarantee for our trouble. "*Yet faith is the substance of things hoped for and the evidence of things not seen* (Hebrews 11:1).

Faith is essential to salvation, faith is the crux on which our trust, hope, and assurance relies. The concept of faith hinges on our ability to hold sure to what we believe even though we cannot visibly see it. Our faith grows and develops out of our conviction and obedience and is built upon experiences and knowledge of God's will for our lives.

We must not view our grief, loss, or inability as punishment and consequences of sin. Refer to these scriptures as sources of strength and encouragement:

John 9:1-3 (NKJV): *"Now as Jesus passed by, He saw a man who was blind from birth. [2] And His disciples asked Him, saying, "Rabbi, who sinned, this man or his parents, that he was born blind?" [3] Jesus answered, "Neither this man nor his parents sinned, but that the works of God should be revealed in him.* This scripture shows Jesus dispelling the Jewish belief of the time that disabilities or deformities were somehow a result of sins committed. Jesus used this occurrence of the blind man's condition as an opportunity to show God's power as an example to the disciples, the blind man, and those who the blind man would share his experience with.

Romans 8:1 (NKJV): "*There is therefore now no condemnation to them which are in Christ Jesus, who walk not after the flesh, but after the Spirit.*"

Matthew 5:45 (KJV): *"That ye may be the children of your Father which is in heaven: for he maketh his sun to rise on the evil and on the good, and sendeth rain on the just and on the unjust."*

Psalm 103:12 (NIV): *"As far as the east is from the west, so far has he removed our transgressions from us"*

If God has taken the time to remind us through scripture several times that He has not only removed the stain of sin from us but has forgotten them completely, it doesn't do us any good to remind ourselves or to hold on to times we've felt like failures. It is just another trick of the enemy used to distract us from the love and compassion God has for us as His children. We must learn to show ourselves that same love and compassion.

Reflect and remind yourself that God is good, and His love is not limited by your situation or condition. Trust Him with the plans and purpose for your life beyond childbearing, beyond your circumstances.

Now, when I look at my scars and reflect on the trials and hardship associated with infertility, I'm reminded that Jesus has scars as well, and His scars saved my life. Not only are His scars evidence of His love for me, but Jesus has kept his nail-scarred hands and feet and pierced side for us to see in glory. The purpose of that is to serve as a reminder of the sacrifice He made to bring us into His family.

One of my favorite scriptures remind me that His wounds healed me. Isaiah 53:5 states, *"But he was wounded for our transgressions, he was bruised for our iniquities, the chastisement of our peace was upon him, and with his stripes we are healed.*"

Psalm 30:11-12a brings me so much peace every time I see, think about, or feel my scars: *"You have turned my mourning into joyful dancing. You have taken away my clothes of mourning and clothed me with joy, that I might sing praises to you and not be silent..."* (NLT)

Faith can only be strengthened by the word of God. It is our source and will always sustain us if allowed. The Word of God is life unto them that finds it and peace to their soul.

Chapter 8
Again, I Say, Wait on The Lord

We have a tendency to want to control every aspect of our lives. We want to dictate and construct how everything will go. By high school, some of us have already mapped our life out, where we will live, what type of career we will have, what kind of car we will drive, the age we will marry, number of kids, etcetera. But God in His infinite wisdom knows best. He is more than capable of handling our lives for His divine purpose and plan. We have to submit to His perfect will for our lives. Not the cookie cutter preconceived world views of what our lives are supposed to look like.

How often do we dwell on our past, our choices, allowing these to fill us with regret and shame? All based upon what we thought was best for our lives. True submission and trust in God relieves us of unrealistic expectations and pressures we have a tendency to take on. Trust God with your dreams and aspirations.

3 John 1:2 states, "*I wish above all things that you may prosper and enjoy good health, as your soul prospers.*" He wants the best for us; He gives us desires and dreams that align with His will for our lives. Seeking Him in all things takes the undue pressure and strain of trying to conform and fit into standards and values determined by the world.

Whether cultural, societal, racial, gender, ethnocentric, etcetera, we can be influenced and shaped by these. That's why we must know who we are in Christ and accept God's truth that our value doesn't come from worldly standards but from His love for us through His death and resurrection.

God has a heart for the lowly, unworthy, the downtrodden, the outcasts of life. He's always interceding, seeking to dwell with us, waiting to be invited in. He values those who are meek and admit their reliance and need for Him. Scripture shows us this. We can be vulnerable, open, and honest with the Savior. He is waiting for a fresh encounter with you.

During your season of waiting, what is God asking of you? Is it to stay focused on His faithfulness towards you? Is He attempting to strengthen your faith in His Word? To draw you nearer through personal study time? Or is it to simply strengthen your faith in that He hears your prayers? The simple yet powerful truth is that faith comes by hearing and hearing by the Word of God (Romans 10:17). Take this time to purposefully seek the Lord; carve specific and intentional prayer and study time. The Word of God is life; a living, breathing source for sustainment and nourishment to our parched, hungry souls.

Reflect on periods of waiting and how God orchestrates every detail for your growth. Waiting is counterintuitive to what the world holds as normal; instinctively, we want everything immediately. We live in a fast paced technologically advanced society. A microwave, in and out, I-Want-It-Now mentality. We're no longer accustomed to waiting on anything. Tablets, cellphones, laptops, and gadgets of the like are touted to increase our productivity and efficiency all over lightning speed Wi-Fi. Communication companies build brands and its customer base on their promise of the fastest downloads in the shortest time. Grocery stores have self-check kiosks and are offering online shopping and delivery because no one wants to wait on a cashier. You can receive purchases shipped from across the world within a day's time. And with the allure of a quick response, instant messaging and text have become a part of the norm for communicating.

But ironically with this shift in culture and the ever advancement of technology, we've become more disconnected and impatient. I'm mindful that I don't know anyone who enjoys waiting. And though waiting is a part of life, it's often viewed negatively and as something to avoid if at all possible. But how are we making the best use of that time? What are we doing while waiting?

Think of a time you noticed a group of friends and no one was talking because their eyes were glued to their smartphones. Or consider the amount of time actually spent holding a conversation while waiting for seating at a restaurant or on the preparation of your food order. Are we using the time wisely by sharing and conversing with our friends and relatives which in turn builds empathy and intimacy with others? Or, as studies have shown, are we becoming more and more disconnected? What we do with the time we have even in waiting is important not only for our relationships with friends and family but with God.

Modern technology feeds our impatience and expectations of instant gratification. We want everything quick, fast, and in a hurry. Truth be told, we come to God with these same expectations. We pray and expect an instant response, an immediate answer to our petitions. And because technology caters to these worldly desires, we in turn require them of God. Then when or if we don't receive immediate answers, we perceive God as uncaring, or we attempt to handle things on our own.

But, My Dear Sister, God does not conform to the standards and ways of this world. He is Holy and sovereign and cannot be moved. He hears every prayer and answers according to His will. As a consequence, when we begin to understand and accept this, we begin to see God working in us while we are waiting on Him with expectation. As such, we come to realize that sometimes the process is just as important as the result.

"Coming before God in quietness and waiting upon Him in silence often can accomplish more than days of feverish activity."—AW Tozer

Personal testimony: Once I realized my "why" and became intentional about living gratefully for the many blessings and good in my life in spite of my pain, I went from impatience to peace, from a death warrant to life promised to worship and serve God, from hopeless to hopeful, suicidal thoughts to planning and participating, preparing for my future! I'm pregnant with possibilities and birthing dreams and purpose.

I struggled with the fear of not leaving a legacy by not birthing children to share my love with, to train them up in the admonition of the Lord, to teach them what my parents taught me. I could not believe that I would not have the opportunity to teach my future generations about my parents and the love of God.

But God reminded me that childbearing is not the only way to leave a legacy. That by sharing my pain, sharing my testimony of how God healed my heart, how He restored my joy, how He lifted my head and snatched me from the grips of depression and despair through His love *is* legacy building.

If I can save one woman, one couple from the lies of the enemy through encouragement and EXPECTING God to use you and move in your life despite the pain and stigma associated with infertility, then my legacy is fulfilled! I encourage you to hold on and to seek God's sovereign will for your life. His constant, consistent, faithful, relentless love for us is astounding, and God's timing and perfect will for our lives is amazingly beautiful.

Chapter 9
Expecting

"[17] Although the fig tree shall not blossom, neither shall fruit be in the vines; the labour of the olive shall fail, and the fields shall yield no meat; the flock shall be cut off from the fold, and there shall be no herd in the stalls: [18] Yet I will rejoice in the LORD, I will joy in the God of my salvation. [19] The LORD God is my strength, and he will make my feet like hinds' feet, and he will make me to walk upon mine high places…" Habakkuk 3:17-19 (KJV)

God whispered to me, "Who do you say that I am? I want to birth something in you just as life changing. Something I intend for you to nurture, take care of, protect, and love. For I know the thoughts I have for you. Thoughts of peace and not of evil to give you an expected end."

I have to be honest. I was not receptive to God at that point. I was so angry. I said, "I can't believe you're asking me to do something. I asked you for a child, for a family of my own. I've done everything you've told me to do. I've been obedient to your Word. I'm active in my church and ministry, and what has it gotten me?" I felt I sacrificed my fertility, my years of viability, my child bearing years waiting on God, waiting for Him to send my husband, to live the covenant life/ promise of the Bible.

Then God led me to 1 Kings 19:11-14 when God spoke to Elijah in the still small voice, instead of the wind and earthquake. Often, we want God to bless to us in ways that are bold and immediate, in ways that are more comfortable for us. Blessings come in many various forms. God speaks in different ways. God used my inability to conceive to bring me closer to Him and as a testimony of His grace, power, and love. This passage has been a source of strength and encouragement for me to use as an illustration of God not coming or blessing me in the way I expected, but of God's divine plan and Kingdom purpose for my life which is to point others to Him.

I told God, "Lord, I'm broken and empty. I don't want to do anything but wallow in my grief. How am I supposed to move beyond this overwhelming desire that I have? The desire that I believe comes from you. Why would you give me the desire for children to not allow me to have any? What am I to learn from this? What am I to do with these feelings? The hurt, anger, shame, and rejection I've felt for so long. How am I to live with the promise that "All things work together for my good" and "In Christ I am complete" when my heart is broken and I can't see past my tears?"

I began to place my broken heart piece by piece in the Potter's hands. Fragments singed with words like "rejected", "unworthy", "damaged", and "not good enough" all collected from past relationships, heartbreak, disappointments, and unmet expectations. Each piece chipped away and sold with the hopes of a dream come true and repurchased by the Potter with the price paid on the cross.

God wanted to birth something in me that was just as life changing, just as exciting that also had the ability to keep me up at night, wake me up earlier than I wanted to be, and something I needed to nurture, feed, take care of, protect, and love! His divine Kingdom purpose He established for me before my conception.

I can honestly say I've been expecting for years, laboring with the thoughts and visions of ministering to women through the Word of God. Wrestling with the idea, feeling it growing inside my heart year after year; yet, ignoring it. My rationale was I wanted my needs and prayers answered first. I was ignoring the thoughts of ministering to women because I couldn't see myself ministering about something I had no personal experience with.

I was disregarding it because essentially, I was angry with God. Disappointed that I wasn't pregnant with children I'd prayed for in advance, named in advance, purchased clothes in varying sizes, and dreamed of how each would look. Believing in my faith through actions would show God I believed and was preparing to birth my children.

But after each doctor's visit, each surgery, procedure, and test to improve my fertility, I became more and more insolent, frustrated, and disappointed in my body, in my choices, and in my faith. By the time I was in my mid-forties, my doctor told me that I was no longer ovulating, no longer producing eggs to be fertilized. All of these instances led to me asking God, "Why? Why should I do what you want, God? I've done my part. I've praised you, worshipped you, put my faith into action. Yet, I can't get pregnant! So you haven't done your part; I've kept my end of the bargain." As if we can really have anything to bargain with God. Silly me.

Plus, I don't want to tell the world I'm infertile. But if I answer the call to minister to women, I have to be completely transparent with the most shameful thing I've ever dealt with. I'm a single, childless woman in my early fifties, God! In my anger I asked God, "What other statistic do you want to add to my life like a tagline?"

How can I encourage and minister to women who are probably dealing with issues of raising children or experiencing marriage problems when I cannot relate on a personal level to their concerns? What can I tell a woman who is going through something I have never dealt with?

God said, "Tell them to trust me."

The message is the same for everyone, no matter what the issue is you're facing, your status, or situation. TRUST God.

"Tell them to trust me with their children, and to seek me for direction in their marriage." Proverbs 3:5-6 (KJV) says, *"5 Trust in the LORD with all thine heart; and lean not unto thine own understanding. 6 In all thy ways acknowledge him, and he shall direct thy paths."*

God reminded me again, "Tell them of the story of Elijah in 1 Kings where Elijah remained faithful through years of drought, depression, and discouragement, and after defeating the prophets of Baal on Mount Carmel. Remind them when I told Ahab go eat and drink for there is a SOUND of abundant rain."

Elijah sent his servant seven times looking for rain. On the seventh time, the servant said there "arise a little cloud about the size of a man's hand out of the sea" (1 Kings 18:44). I asked myself why God would require Elijah to pray and look seven times before the rain He previously promised arrived.

Personal reflection: Have you prayed or waited for something for a long season? Has God given you an indication no matter how small? Or allowed you a glimpse that He is working?

Think about this: you've already won the victory. The adversaries attempt to keep you depressed and distressed is a ploy to shift your focus from God. Scripture says, "Though the vision tarry wait on it, for at the appointed time it will come to pass" (Habakkuk

2:3). God's Word does not return void; it will do what he says it will do: *"So shall my word be that goeth forth out of my mouth: it shall not return unto me void, but it shall accomplish that which I please, and it shall prosper in the thing whereto I sent it"* Isaiah 55:11 (KJV).

Elijah continued to look in expectation of the rain *while* he was praying. God had already told him the famine and drought would last three years. Yet Elijah still had to pray in faith and ask God to let it rain *then*. Yes, the three years had come. And yes, God in his sovereignty could have ended the drought in Israel and caused the rain to fall earlier. But during those three years, there was still purpose. God always has a Kingdom plan. As we discussed in earlier chapters, the widow of Zarephath's faith was tested as she was making ready the last meal for her and her son when Elijah asked her to cook his meal first. That was purpose.

Question: Did she waiver because her blessing took longer to come than she thought? God had already told her a prophet would come; yet, she was preparing to die. Was it because perhaps it came differently than she expected? Why waiver when God had prepared the way for her and her son to survive the famine and drought even before Elijah arrived? Our behavior and belief during the *meantime* is tantamount to our faith *in* God.

What's your *in the meantime*? What is your *why*?

What do you do while you're waiting? When your prayers seem like they're bouncing off the walls and you're talking to yourself? When the answer you're waiting on hasn't come? When you feel like God has forgotten about the very thing he spoke into your spirit? When it gets harder and harder to dream because your dreams are heavy with the weight of expectation? When your day turns into dark nights and midnight is all day? When there is no cloud in the sky and not even the smell of rain? How do you hold on to the promise? What is your reason, your why for holding on to the promise?

There was a season where I began asking God to do something new in my life. I told Him I wanted to be excited about something again; I wanted something to look forward to. I needed a new venture, job, a hobby, a new relationship, a reason to hold on. Honestly, I was asking God for a new promise, a new purpose because I *felt* the promises and life purpose He'd placed in my heart years ago were taking too long to come forth. Were too painful and filled with failure and regret, and I did not have the strength, courage, and faith to hold on. I argued within myself that I must have misinterpreted what He said, my heart's dream, this longing, often overwhelming desire to birth children and have a husband and family must have come from my own selfish desires. Or maybe I was just going along with societal norms and expectations of womanhood that was plastered on billboards, magazine covers, in fairy tales, on television, and movies.

Yes. That had to be it because God wouldn't— He couldn't— be taking **this** long to respond and to grant what He had purposed in my heart when days had turned into weeks, weeks to months, months into years. So, I'm quitting. I'm giving up. I'm asking for a do over. Mattox has thrown in the proverbial white flag. I'm done dreaming.

Then one day while reading a devotional, I was again reminded of my true purpose: "[27] *So God created man in his own image, in the image of God created he him; male and female created he them.* [28] *And God blessed them, and God said unto them, Be fruitful, and multiply, and replenish the earth, and subdue it: and have dominion over the fish of the sea, and over the fowl of the air, and over every living thing that moveth upon the earth"* (Genesis 1:27-28 (KJV)).

I can't tell you how many times I've read this scripture. The number of times I've prayed and quoted it back to God all while reminding Him, "This is what you said to do, Lord! This is why you created me. So what's the hold up? I'm willing and ready."

And it hit me! It was if God said, "No, My Child, what are YOU waiting on? My purpose and plans have not changed, just as I told Adam and Eve in the Garden and every man and woman since. I'm the same yesterday and today. I assigned your purpose and value at creation."

I was created to praise God, to worship Him for who He is, to bring glory to His name. To "be fruitful and multiply", to plant seeds of His love, to produce disciples, to spread the joy of my salvation. To birth His undying ever faithful love in a generation of women who have felt the sting of disappointment, who are wrestling with hopes unfulfilled, struggling in their attempts of seeking acceptance of the world's value purchased with the currency of status symbols, beauty standards, wealth, body shaming, material wealth, ethnicity, and so on.

In the interim, do what you were designed and purposed to do. God has a plan and a purpose for everything even during the suffering, unfairness, life moments of silence, and unanswered prayers. Recall His goodness, recall His promises, remember who you are in Him, and hold on to His unfailing love.

As mentioned prior, Hebrews 11:1 states, *"Now faith is the substance of things hoped for, the evidence of things not seen."* In different parts of the Bible, men and women who were termed faithful were those who chose to trust in God against all odds and varying situations. You might not find the need to trust in God if you are not in a difficult or challenging situation. I am not saying that it is only in an uncomfortable state that we must trust the Lord, but I often say you don't know who all God is until you need Him to be all that He is!

It was persecution that made the apostles spread out of Jerusalem to propagate the gospel. The more the persecution, the more the trust and increase in faith.

Your faith becomes watered and less potent if based only on words. Strife and testing of faith is what grows our faith and our dependence on God.

"You can't live through what you haven't experienced" is the logic of life. If you've never endured hardship, you won't know what the other side of overcoming and triumph look like. You must go through some heartache to experience God's faithfulness.

The patriarchs continued to believe in God when there was little sign of hope. There had not been any experience of rain before the calling of Noah, yet Noah believed everything from the Lord. Abram was in a situation where he was asked to leave his home, his family, and everything he was familiar with for an unknown place. Abram did so without looking back and doubting God, despite the human tendency we all have to do just that. To wonder, *Is this what you really meant? Are you sure, God?* Furthermore, Abram believed God for a child, not considering the age of his body and the deadness of Sarai's.

The faithful all lived above fear and challenges because they had strong belief in God's Word. The only weapon they used was faith in the Word of God and prayers. Like them, we will be tested, but our hope must be alive in God, and our faith must stand the test of time. Time is a revealer of your true identity and a tester of faith.

Mothers of faith were never put to shame or their

prayers left unanswered. Sarai was old, but she gave birth to the lineage from which the salvation of man came from. Even when God promised her a child at an old age, she looked at her physical body and asked herself how a woman who has stopped menstruating for years give birth. The Bible says she laughed, thinking it was impossible. But He is God. He only needs something to build upon, and that is our faith. He called those things which were not as though they were. Our God is alive to do the same thing of old in your life. He is the same yesterday, today and forever.

Hannah was frustrated to that unimaginable level, but what was birthed from her was a complete blessing to God. Her son Samuel became one of the greatest prophets and proponents of the faith of mankind.

Time will not permit me to talk about the other examples of Saints in the Bible who held on to their faith, who fought the good fight in perilous times of persecution and tribulations. The good news is that all received what was promised even though it might have taken longer than expected.

Please know I am in no way telling you that your grief is minimal or something to be dismissed. And I'm definitely not telling you to get over it. Everyone has their own grieving process, and I'm not at all presuming to know where you are in yours. My prayer is that the love of God will be a reminder that we can move forward in faith with Him. He is the lifter of our heads and our healer if we allow Him.

Matthew 11:28-30 KJV states, *"[28] Come unto me, all ye that labour and are heavy laden, and I will give you rest. [29] Take my yoke upon you, and learn of me; for I am meek and lowly in heart: and ye shall find rest unto your souls. [30] For my yoke is easy, and my burden is light."*

We don't have to carry the burden of infertility and loneliness alone. We have a Father and Savior who understands, are aware, and are willing and able to help us in our time of need. They know how much we can bear and are a restorer of our joy when our faith is low and will pick us up and give us a new song. Every struggle, every heartache, every tear, every sleepless night, every moment of loneliness, every trial and test, every negative result and disappointment, *They* know!

The Lord is an ever present help. He is willing to come to our aid, but we must trust and lean upon Him. The enemy wants us to run from God in our times of distress, to deny His love for us, to turn away from the truth. John 10:10 says, *"The enemy comes but to kill, steal, and destroy..."* That's his sole purpose, and he is bent on doing just that by any means necessary. He will use any tactic, pain, illness, diagnosis, hurt, anger, frustration, anything that he feels he can use as a foothold to cause us to question God's unyielding love for us and His infinite wisdom. His ultimate goal is to keep us bound and insecure of our wholeness while attempting to destroy our relationship with Christ.

I've talked about being infertile in the medical sense of being unable to conceive and get pregnant; however, I would be remiss if I didn't acknowledge that we can be infertile and/or barren in ways that aren't medical. We can become unproductive and unfruitful in our relationship with Christ, stagnate in the use of our gifts and talents, bogged down with frustration and complacency that can come with life's disappointments.

I want to encourage you to press toward the mark in Jesus Christ. Become determined to go higher in God and stir up your faith. Healing and restoration are in Him, and God is able to birth something great in your life for His plans and purpose. That stronghold that the enemy is using to keep you bound in grief, fear, and pain doesn't have to be your reality.

Say this after me: I break the yoke of infertility. I break the yoke of barrenness. For greater is He that is in me than he that is in the world. I'm complete in the Lord Jesus. I may be barren physically, but not spiritually. The earth is the Lord and the fullness thereof, so my quiver is full of God's heritage. I'm a joint heir with Christ Jesus, and my land shall no more be called barren because I am delighted of God.

Losing your expectation causes you to lose your potential for a miracle. Expect God to do great things in your life. Expect Him to turn your mourning into singing, your pain into Kingdom purpose, and expect Him to love you through it. Philippians 1:6 offers the comfort of "*I am convinced and confident of this very thing, that He who has begun a good work in you will continue to perfect and complete it until the day of Jesus Christ.*"

Oh, ye Barren, listen. I've had to comfort myself with these very words while remembering the testament of women of old who kept the hope through their faith. Though the promise seems to have grown old, our father in heaven can't promise what He will not do. His word will not return void. He did not forget them even though they may have felt forgotten or even ridiculed. Yet, the precious name God called them— the name of Daughter, Beautiful, Favored, Fruitful, etcetera— stood the test of time and serves as a testament to His love and faithfulness.

These heroes and heroines of faith never believed what they saw or the insults of man more than the word of God. But rather they ran into their prayer closet and sought what God had said in His word concerning their situation. We should use their example. They all lived above fear and challenges because they gave themselves to God's words and fervent prayers. Not weak in faith, but reverent in the spirit, serving the Lord. The only weapon they used was faith in the Word of God and prayers. These staunch women of faith held on to the scripture and promises of the Most High.

Chapter 10
Rebirth

Can I be transparent? I know, I know. You're probably saying, "How much more transparent are you going to be? How many more closely held secret issues are you going to share?" Well, as many as I need to in an effort to show how broken, fractured, and frazzled I am, and how the most amazing God, the creator of the entire universe who whispered my name before I was even a thought, cherishes and loves me unequivocally without hesitation. And the good news is He loves you just as much, too!

So here goes.

Time has recently become my greatest enemy, taunting me in the mirror with every fine line and grey hair. Lurking around every corner in every young woman's face reminding me that time is slipping away. Filling even the smallest crevice with "should have", "wish I'd", "if only", and "what ifs".

It's amazing how loud the formidable, undefeated, undisputed champion Mother Biological Clock can be. How can she be internally silent, yet chime, clang, bang, and make her presence known with such a resounding potency and force of biological proportions that leaves no doubt of her onset and subsequent arrival? She has surely faced many opponents; she has stood the test of centuries and decades. Yet her only true challenger is Father Time.

I remember as a youth wishing time away. Saying things like "I can't wait to grow up", "I wish I could drive", "I'm so ready to be out of high school". Now I'm more reflective and wondering where did the time go? I'm reminded of the lyrics of "Fly Like an Eagle" by the Steve Miller Band, "Time keeps on slipping, slipping, slipping into the future." Time, one of the most valuable things we want, yet can't buy, is wasted and cherished at the same time.

Yet, honestly, I've spent very little time in the present. Big SIGH. There, I said it. Now let me explain.

Seems like I've always lived for the whens or somedays of life. In the past, it was "when I grow up", 'when I start driving", "when I graduate high school", "when I graduate college". Now it's "when I get married", "when I have children", "when I lose weight", "when I retire", on and on and on.

Oh, I'm alive, but I've not lived. Lived for the moments, lived for the here and nows, nor lived to seize the day. I've often felt my life will truly begin *someday*, and that *someday* has been attached to me reaching the perfect dress size, making more money, having my dream job, a husband and family. Or when I've paid off all my student loans. Now that will be a huge sigh of relief!

Don't get me wrong. My life is good. I've traveled some, have the love and support of my family, a great group of friends who I laugh and share with often. I enjoy many of the comforts of life, have more than I need, and some great memories that will serve me for a lifetime. Yet, if I'm truly honest, there's always been a...."but". I've felt like, "Yes, things are good, **but** they'll be so much better when..."

Maybe you can relate. Maybe your someday is "when the kids are older" or "when they go off to college" or "when I make more money" or "when I get a house", or "when I finish school", "when I move", "when I finish a personal goal", "when I retire".

Can I share with you my wakeup call? Life was passing me by, and I realized in all probability I had more life behind me than in front. My dear sister, anything that prohibits you from living for and in the present is robbing you of just that— your present. Today is a gift, uniquely wrapped and hand delivered to us from God. Each day is not promised, but each day holds so much promise. Think of each minute with an eternal perspective, not as a temporary place card that is to be glossed over for the unknown future.

In every minute of the day, I have to choose to trust God just as much with my future as I do with my right now and learn to live in the very moments that He's blessed me to see. Each day holds 1,440 minutes never to be repeated again.

Think about this. How you take care of and cherish your current assignment might determine your next assignment. And when you're faithful over the small things, it strengthens and prepares you for greater things (Luke 16:10).

I think we can agree that childbearing is God's design for women. We were uniquely created biologically to reproduce. The emotional essence of a woman is one of nurturers and cultivators which I believe is by design as well, and scripture tells us to be fruitful and multiply. The creation and continuation of life mandate given to Mother Eve and carried out to this day addresses the role women and mothers have played since the beginning of time. Whether you've birthed a child(ren) or you have served as a mother figure, the role of nurturing, cultivating, and supporting remains the same.

In my opinion, as women, we "birth" all the time. We birth friendships and relationships that last a lifetime. We birth new ideas and gifts and talents within ourselves and each other daily. We birth joy and love and hearts of gratitude. We birth extraordinary opportunities to create things that are out of the box or out of the norm. Just look at all of the female entrepreneurs or mompreneurs who have conceived ways and techniques to make life, products, or motherhood and child rearing easier.

And most of all, we birth relationships with our Lord and Savior Jesus Christ. In some cases, we may introduce our children, friends, family, and coworkers to Him; in other cases, we strengthen or solidify their relationship with our Father through our testimony, how we live, how we handle life's challenges and trials. Yes, we are fruitful, and we produce and multiply in so many ways, in so many instances.

Take heart, my sister-friend whether you are like me and struggling with infertility and all the emotions and feelings attached to the diagnosis, or you are in a stage of your life wondering what God's plans and Kingdom purposes specifically for you. Whatever your status— single, married, divorced, widowed, mother, or mother figure— just remember He is faithful and just, He loves you, He thinks of you often, and He calls you amazing. There is no one else able to do what He has purposed for you to do. There is no back up plan, no plan B in case it doesn't work. Your life now, the time you've been given, the skills and talents He's blessed you with are all for this lifetime.

Chapter 11
Repurpose Your Pain

Like most items, there may be a time limit or shelf life placed on its longevity for when it is considered beyond its prime or has reached an expiration date. For instance, food or household products all have expiration dates placed on them. Webster's Dictionary defines expire as "to come to an end; terminate, as a contract, guarantee, or offer".

As women, there can be several seasons in our lives where we are defined by time: puberty, adolescence, young adulthood, marriage, childbearing years, menopause, divorce, empty nester, retirement, etcetera. And as such, there may be moments of time when we find ourselves wondering what's next and what is the purpose found in this season of life? You may feel as if you have been given an EXPIRATION date or marked as EXPIRED. Your time has passed, value diminished, no longer considered valuable or worthy. However, our purpose is found in God. Since we are an extension of Him and a joint heir with Christ, our divine purpose is to proclaim the good news of His love and abounding grace.

During these times, draw closer to God, and consider sharing your journey with someone. I'm sure there is wisdom to be offered. Someone needs to know how you made it over. Someone needs to know what you did to survive or trudge through that period of singleness, divorce, widowhood, death, childrearing, retirement etcetera. Everything is useful. God does not waste a tear, an experience, a situation, a trial, nor a test. There is nothing He cannot use for His glory.

You may feel there isn't anything worth salvaging, nothing that can be used from your trial, and that there is nothing to offer from your tears. But remember we give birth all the time. We give birth to our thoughts, good or bad; therefore, we can turn any situation, any pain, and every life experience into a useful instrument of repurpose.

I must admit I'm not a creative, artsy-crafty type girl. I've never been particularly good at sewing or creating or making things from scratch. Listen. I have difficulty cutting a straight line with a pair of scissors, so you definitely don't want me to handle a glue gun! Yet, I find the Do-It-Yourself, remodeling, renovating channel craze fascinating.

I'm sure you are aware of the trend. Most shows start by introducing you to individuals and couples who have purchased their first home or second home, and it's usually a fixer upper. The show follows their story as they go to great lengths to restore or remodel the new home. Oftentimes, you will find where the new owners will reuse some of the original framework, flooring, or fixtures. Not just in an attempt to save money, but because there is still usefulness in the object. Though it may have some dents, showing effects of aging, and quite possibly requiring some cleaning to remove years of wear and tear, in the eye of the beholder, there is still beauty to be found. Sometimes, the original is found hidden behind or underneath something. Maybe it was covered up for some reason, or at the time it was no longer needed.

I recall an episode where at some point in the ownership of the home, the original wooden flooring had been covered with carpeting, and the new owners had no idea until it was decided to replace the carpet and update it with new contemporary flooring. Upon realizing that some places of the wooden floor were worn and rotten and that all of the floor could not be retained, it was decided to remove the wooden floor and go with the initial idea of a completely new floor. However, the contractor and host of the show suggested restoring several areas and sections of the wooden floor for a completely different use. In the end, they had cabinet doors, a counter top, and a coffee table all made from the repurposed wooden floors.

God is willing to do the same thing with your pain, tears, and trials. You're feeling forgotten, neglected, overlooked, misused, abandoned… Maybe you feel past your prime, or you're in a season of wondering what's next. Allow God to refurbish, restore, and repurpose your pain. He can do so much more with it than you can. Allow Him to bring you into a space of peace and contentment in Him. Let Him use you to help someone else going through the same thing. Let

Him birth a testimony; let Him birth a new thing. Isaiah 43:18-19 KJV states, *"18 Remember ye not the former things, neither consider the things of old. 19 Behold, I will do a new thing; now it shall spring forth; shall ye not know it? I will even make a way in the wilderness, and rivers in the desert."*

Consider going back to school, starting that new business you've been dreaming about. Why not travel to new places, learn a different language, adopt or foster a child, or learn and start a new hobby?

The joy of the Lord will be with you and will be your strength.

What can we say when our faith seems to produce no result and our enemy is daily mocking and disgracing the identity that God gave us? The simple and powerful answers to this undeniable heart felt situations are imbedded in two things:

- Strengthen your faith in the Word of God
- Strengthen your faith in prayers

Stop mourning for your loss but rather stir up your faith and the gifts God has placed in you. Again, say this after me: "I break the yoke of infertility. For greater is He that is in me than he than he that is in the world. I'm complete in the Lord Jesus, so I can't be barren. The earth is the Lord and the fullness thereof."

Finally, can we say this together: “My God is able to do exceedingly abundantly above all we can think or ask according to the power that wrought in us.”

Amen.

Thank you for reading! Please leave a book review wherever you can.

Made 4 This
Publishing

Mrs Audrey

my adopted mother

Thanks for always showing concern and taking care of your "adopted daughter" and for your prayers, love and encouragement!

God's continued Blessing

Ragitt

II Corin 1:3-4

Made in the USA
Columbia, SC
11 February 2022

55868985R00050